Kyna Duquet • Anna Lombardos • Lina Mailhot

Little Rascal Time

Student Book B

English as a
Second Language,
Elementary
Cycle One

LES ÉDITIONS CEC
Une compagnie de Quebecor Media

9001, boul. Louis-H.-La Fontaine, Anjou (Québec) Canada H1J 2C5
Téléphone : 514-351-6010 • Télécopieur : 514-351-3534

Editorial Manager, ESL
Carolyn Faust

Production Manager
Danielle Latendresse

Production Coordinator
Louise Chabot

Project Editors
Angel Beyde
Nancy Schmidt

Proofreader
Joseph Shragge

Rights Research
Shona French

Cover and Page Design
2NSB

Illustrators
Pierre Berthiaume
Stéphane J. Bourrelle
Michel Grant

About the Authors

Kyna Duquet, Anna Lombardos, and Lina Mailhot have combined many years of experience in the fields of writing and teaching English as a second language with passion and dedication toward children's education.

Acknowledgements

We would like to express sincere thanks to everyone at Les Éditions CEC inc. and Emmanuelle Bruno for the opportunity to be part of such a wonderful team. Our most heartfelt thanks goes to Carolyn Faust, who respectfully guided us with her vision, commitment, and boundless energy. We are grateful for the outstanding editorial work of Angel Beyde; her contribution and encouragement have been invaluable. We also appreciate the work and dedication of Danielle Latendresse, and we applaud 2NSB for beautifully illustrating our words. A big thank you to Iolanda Bolduc, whose experience and guidance helped enrich the quality of the project.

We are thankful to our family and friends and especially to George, Jeff, and Marc-André for their support and understanding. Clara, Tyson, Dylan, Sam, and Dean: you are an infinite source of inspiration!

Text Credits

Page 37
Song Title: HOT POTATO
Composers: M. Cook, J. Fatt, A. Field, G. Page, J. Field
Publisher: Wiggly Tunes Pty. Ltd.

Page 38
Song Title: FRUIT SALAD
Composers: M. Cook, J. Fatt, A. Field, G. Page
Publisher: Wiggly Tunes Pty. Ltd.

Les Éditions CEC remercient le gouvernement du Québec pour l'aide financière apportée à l'édition de cet ouvrage par l'entremise du Programme de crédit d'impôt pour l'édition de livres, administré par la SODEC.

· Table of Contents ·

Lettre aux parents

Cette année, la collection *Little Rascal Time* amènera votre enfant plus loin dans sa découverte de l'anglais. Conçue dans l'esprit du programme d'anglais langue seconde du 1er cycle du primaire, *Little Rascal Time* met l'accent sur la dimension orale de la langue avec des comptines, des chansons et des histoires du répertoire anglophone.

Conformément au programme, le matériel du premier cycle ne vise ni l'apprentissage de la lecture ou de l'écriture mais favorise plutôt le développement de l'écoute et de la communication orale. Tout au long de l'année, votre enfant aura donc l'occasion d'écouter des textes et des chansons qui lui seront lus et chantés, et de participer activement à des activités, que ce soit en répétant des mots, des parties d'histoire ou encore en mimant et en chantant. Cela lui permettra non seulement de se familiariser avec la langue anglaise mais aussi d'acquérir un vocabulaire. Tout ça dans le but de l'encourager à s'exprimer en anglais.

La collection *Little Rascal Time*, en plus d'un manuel de l'élève (*Student Book*), propose des composantes conçues pour soutenir l'intérêt de l'élève et rendre l'enseignement de l'anglais dynamique: du matériel audio et vidéo, des affiches, des jeux et des grands livres d'histoires.

Le manuel de l'élève regroupe l'ensemble des histoires, des chansons et des comptines vues en classe. À la maison, invitez votre enfant à vous démontrer sa compréhension des textes présentés avec des gestes et des mots. Vous pourrez ainsi constater et apprécier sa progression dans l'apprentissage de l'anglais. L'encourager dans cette démarche, lui faire répéter des mots et des phrases, ou encore l'écouter chanter en anglais ne sont que quelques moyens pour l'aider à développer ses compétences en anglais langue seconde.

**Nous souhaitons à votre enfant, ainsi qu'à vous,
de belles découvertes et une bonne année scolaire !**

Letter to the Parents

This year, the *Little Rascal Time* collection will accompany your children as they continue to explore the English language. Developed in line with the English Second Language Program for Cycle One elementary, *Little Rascal Time* focuses on the oral aspect of the language through the use of authentic English stories, rhymes and songs.

In accordance with the Cycle One Program, the collection does not target the learning of reading or writing, but rather targets the development of listening skills and oral communication. Throughout the year, your children will be listening to texts and songs that will be read or sung, and will actively participate in fun activities: repeating words, parts of stories, singing, and doing actions to songs and rhymes. Doing so will help your children to not only become familiar with the English language, but also acquire vocabulary. The goal of this approach is to encourage your children to begin expressing themselves in English.

Beyond the Student Book, the *Little Rascal Time* collection offers additional support material, designed to stimulate the students' interest and facilitate a dynamic teaching approach to English: audio and video material, posters, picture cards, games, and Big Books.

The Student Book is an anthology of all the stories, songs, and rhymes seen in class. At home, we encourage you to invite your children to show you their understanding of these texts through the use of gestures and words. In doing so, you will be able to see for yourself their progress in learning English. Encouraging your children by having them repeat the words or sentences, or even by listening to them sing in English, are just a few ways to help them develop competency in English as a second language.

**We wish your children, and you,
a wonderful adventure in English, as well as a successful,
happy school year!**

My Strategies

I try.

I use resources.

I look.

I cooperate.

I move.

I guess.

I remember.

I show.

I practise.

I ask for help.

I predict.

I self-monitor.
I self-evaluate.

My Competencies

Competency 1: To act on understanding of texts

I explore.

Down by the bay.

I show.

I monitor my learning.

Competency 2: To communicate orally in English

I listen.

I can help!

I say.

I monitor my learning.

I Shine

I show.

I say. Hello!

I look.

I try.

Star Light

Star light,
Star bright,
First star
I see tonight,
I wish I may,
I wish I might,
Have the wish
I wish tonight.

Simon makes a
really long birthday wish list.

Simon makes a really, REALLY long
birthday wish list.

Star light,
Star bright,
First star
I see tonight,
I wish I may,
I wish I might,
Have the wish
I wish tonight.

Simon wishes really hard.

Star light,
Star bright,
First star
I see tonight,
I wish I may,
I wish I might,
Have the wish
I wish tonight.

Simon wishes really, REALLY hard.

Wow! The wish really works!

Wow! The wish really, REALLY works!

So Simon and his family move to a
really big house.

Simon and his family move
to a really, REALLY big house.

"I really miss my friends."

"I really, REALLY miss my friends."

Star light,
Star bright,
First star
I see tonight,
I wish I may,
I wish I might,
Have the wish
I wish tonight.

Simon wishes really hard again.

14

Simon wishes really, REALLY hard.

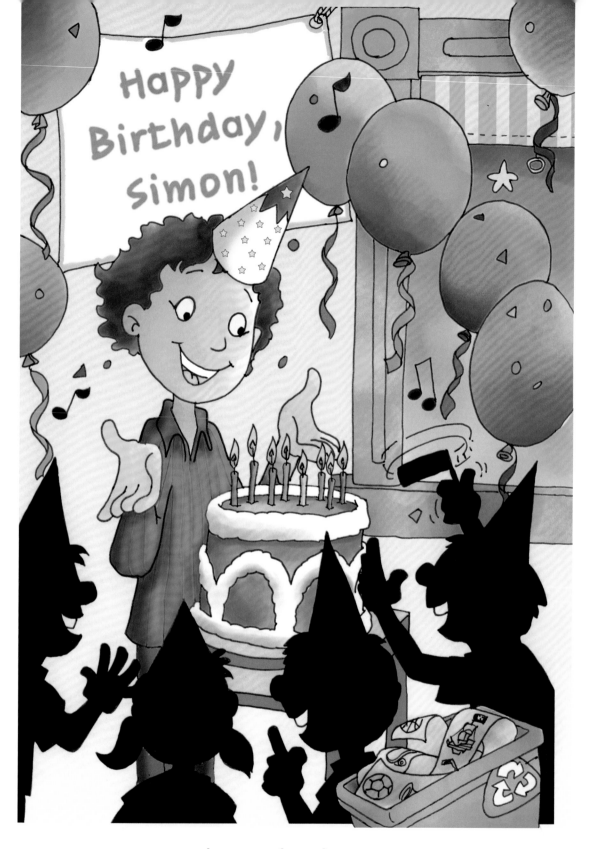

"Welcome back, Simon!
We really missed you."

Star Light, Star Bright

Star  light, star bright,

First star I see  ---- tonight,

I wish  I may, I wish I might,

Have the wish I wish tonight .

Happy Birthday

Happy Birthday to you,

Happy Birthday to you,

Happy Birthday dear Simon,

Happy Birthday to you!

Twinkle, Twinkle Little Star

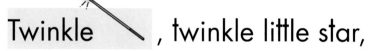

Twinkle , twinkle little star,

How I wonder what you are.

Up above the world so high ,

Like a diamond in the sky .

Twinkle , twinkle little star,

How I wonder what you are.

⭐19

This Little Light of Mine

This little  light of mine,

I'm going to let it shine!

This little light  of mine,

I'm going to let it shine!

This little light of mine ,

I'm going to let it shine!

Let it shine, let it shine, let it shine!

Food, Yummy, Yummy!

I show.

I say. Hello!

I predict.

I use resources.

On Top of Spaghetti

On top of spaghetti,
all covered with cheese,

I lost my poor meatball,
when somebody sneezed.

It rolled off the table
and onto the floor.

And then my poor meatball
rolled out the door.

It rolled down the sidewalk
and under a bush.

And then my poor meatball
was nothing but mush!

The mush was as tasty,
as tasty could be.

And then the next summer,
it grew into a tree.

The tree was all covered,
all covered with moss.

And on it grew meatballs
and tomato sauce.

So if you eat spaghetti,
all covered with cheese,

hold on to your meatball,

whenever you sneeze.

Bless you!

Hot Potato

 Hot potato, hot potato   x2

Hot potato, hot potato

Potato, potato, potato, potato

 Cold spaghetti, cold spaghetti   x2

Cold spaghetti, cold spaghetti

Spaghetti, spaghetti, spaghetti

 Mashed banana, mashed banana   x2

Mashed banana, mashed banana

Banana, banana, banana

 Oh, wiggly, wiggly

Oh, wiggly, wiggly

Gimme that, gimme that, gimme that food!

Fruit Salad

Fruit salad, yummy, yummy!

Fruit salad, yummy, yummy!

Fruit salad, yummy, yummy!

Yummy, yummy, yummy, yummy, fruit salad.

Who Took the Cookie from the Cookie Jar?

Who took  the cookie from the cookie jar?

Rascal took the cookie from the cookie jar.

Who me?

Yes, you!

Couldn't be!

Then, who?

Pat-a-cake

Pat-a-cake, pat-a-cake,

Baker man .

Bake me a cake

As fast as you can.

Roll it and pat it and

Mark it with a B,

And put it in the oven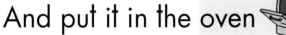

For baby and me!

ABC Song

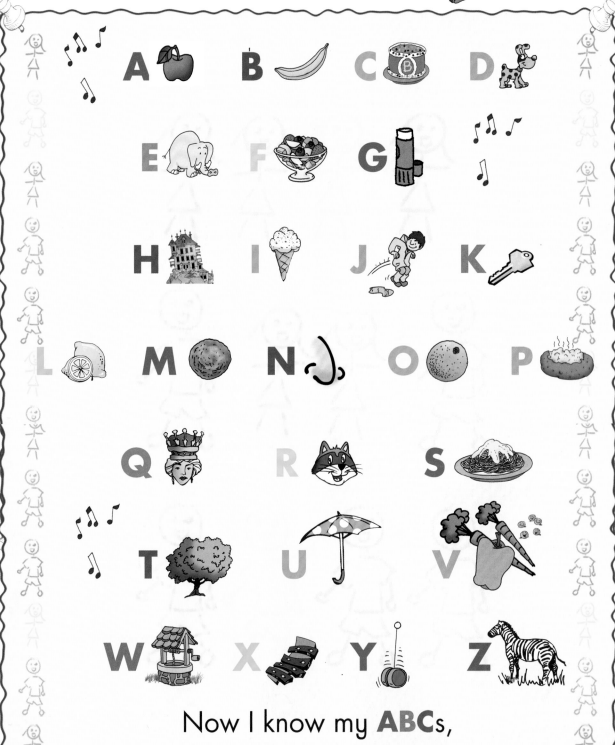

Now I know my **ABC**s,
Next time won't you sing with me?

Ready ...
Set ... Go!

I show.

I say. Hello!

I guess. Star?

I cooperate.

The Tortoise and the Hare

"Look at me. See how fast I run!
Look at me. I am number one!"

"Listen, Hare.
You are fast, it is true.
But I am a champion, too."

"Steady Tortoise, you cannot win this race.
I am always,
ALWAYS in first place!"

Ready, set, GO!

Speedy Hare jumps and talks.
Steady Tortoise walks and walks.

"I am SO fast, I have time to eat."
Speedy Hare enjoys a treat.

"I am SO fast, I have time to play."
Speedy Hare enjoys the day.

"I am SO fast, I have time to sleep."
Speedy Hare rests his feet.

Steady Tortoise does not quit.
Owl cheers him: "You CAN do it!"

"Oh no, oh no!
Where did Steady Tortoise go?"

"There is no time. There is no time.
I have to reach the finish line!"

The end of the race is very near.
All the animals clap and cheer.

"Speedy Hare is in last place.
Steady Tortoise wins the race!"

Slow and steady wins the race!

Two, Four, Six, Eight

Two, four, six, eight!

Who do we appreciate?

Tortoise! Tortoise!

Gooooo Tortoise!

Left Hand, Right Hand

Left hand, left hand,

Reach up high,

Right hand, right hand,

Touch the sky,

Right hand, left hand,

Round, round, round,

Left hand, right hand,

Pound, pound, pound!

Give Me an R!

Give me an <u>R</u>

Give me an <u>A</u>

Give me an <u>S</u>

Give me a <u>C</u>

Give me an <u>A</u>

Give me an <u>L</u>

Gooooo <u>Rascal</u>!

The More We Get Together

Oh, the more we get together ,

Together, together,

Oh, the more we get together,

The happier we'll be.

For your friends are my friends ,

And my friends are your friends.

Oh, the more we get together,

The happier we'll be!

Hooray!

Hip!

Hip!

Hooray!

UNIT **4**

Summer Fun

I show.

I say. Hello!

I cooperate.

I remember.

Down by the bay,
where the watermelons grow,
back to my home, I dare not go,
for if I do, my mother will say ...

"Did you ever see a bee
with a sunburned knee?
Down by the bay!"

Down by the bay,
where the watermelons grow,
back to my home, I dare not go,
for if I do, my mother will say ...

"Did you ever see a whale
with a polka dot tail?
Down by the bay!"

Down by the bay,
where the watermelons grow,
back to my home, I dare not go,
for if I do, my mother will say ...

"Did you ever see a cat
wearing a hat?
Down by the bay!"

Down by the bay,
where the watermelons grow,
back to my home, I dare not go,
for if I do, my mother will say ...

"Did you ever see an ant
eating a plant?
Down by the bay!"

Down by the bay,
where the watermelons grow,
back to my home, I dare not go,
for if I do, my mother will say ...

"Did you ever see a bear
combing her hair?
Down by the bay!"

Down by the bay,
where the watermelons grow,
back to my home, I dare not go,
for if I do, my mother will say ...

"Did you ever see a llama
wearing blue pyjamas?
Down by the bay!"

Down by the bay,
where the watermelons grow,
back to my home, I dare not go,
for if I do, my mother will say ...

"Did you ever see a dragon
pulling a wagon?
Down by the bay!"

Row, Row, Row Your Boat

Row, row, row your boat ,

Gently down the stream  .

Merrily, merrily, merrily, merrily  ,

 Life is but a dream .

4 3 8 9 10

I Caught a Fish Alive

One 1, two 2,

Three 3, four 4, five 5!

Once I caught a fish  alive.

Six 6, seven 7,

Eight 8, nine 9, ten 10!

Then I let it go again.

"Why did you let it go?"

"Because he bit my finger  so."

"Which finger did he bite  ?"

"This little finger on the right  ."

Calamine Lotion

My body needs calamine lotion ,

My body's all **red** you can see.

The flowers I picked

For my mommy,

Turned out to be poison ivy !

Don't touch, don't touch, don't touch

The leaves of three.

Don't touch, don't touch, don't touch

The leaves of three.

Year Round

Three Little Witches

One little, two little, three little witches ,

Fly  over haystacks ,

Fly over ditches 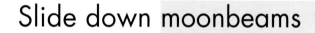,

Slide down moonbeams

Without any hitches,

Hey ho, Halloween's here!

 Trick or Treat

Trick or Treat!

Give me something good to eat!

Halloween Is Coming Soon

Halloween is coming soon,

coming soon, coming soon,

Halloween is coming soon,

Oh, what fun!

Black cats sitting on a fence,

on a fence, on a fence,

Black cats sitting on a fence,

Meow! Meow! Meow!

Owls a-hooting in the trees,

in the trees, in the trees,

Owls a-hooting in the trees,

Whoo! Whoo! Whoo!

Witches flying on their brooms,

on their brooms, on their brooms,

Witches flying on their brooms,

Eee! Eee! Eee!

A Chubby Little Snowman

A chubby little snowman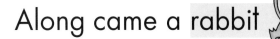

Had a carrot nose .

Along came a rabbit ,

And what do you suppose?

That hungry little bunny ,

Looking for his lunch ,

Ate the snowman's carrot nose …

Nibble, nibble, CRUNCH !

Jingle Bells

Jingle bells, jingle bells,

Jingle all the way.

Oh what fun it is to ride

In a one-horse open sleigh!

Snowflakes

Snowflakes, snowflakes , falling down,

On the trees and on the ground .

I will build a man of snow ,

Tall black hat

and eyes of coal,

If the sun comes out today,

I will watch you melt away!

Roses Are Red

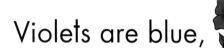

Roses are red,

Violets are blue,

Sugar is sweet,

And so are you.

Counting Valentines

Valentines, valentines, how many do I see?

Valentines, valentines, count them with me.

I have **red** ones, **orange** ones, **yellow** ones, too.

I have **green** ones, **purple** ones,

And some that are **blue**.

Valentines, valentines, how many do I see?

Count them with me! 1-2-3-4-5 …

April

April

April is a rainbow month,

Of sudden springtime showers.

Bright with golden daffodils

And lots of pretty flowers.

Itsy Bitsy Spider

Itsy bitsy spider

Climbed the water spout.

Down came the rain

And washed the spider out!

Out came the sun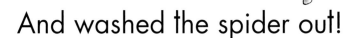

And dried up all the rain.

So itsy bitsy spider climbed up the spout again!

What the Robin Told

The wind

Told the grasses,

And the grasses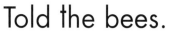

Told the trees.

The trees

Told the bushes,

And the bushes

Told the bees.

The bees

Told the robin,

And the robin

Sang out clear:

Wake up!

Wake up!

Spring is here!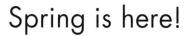